# West Virginia

by Patricia K. Kummer,
Capstone Press
Geography Department

**Content Consultant**:
Allan Hardway
West Virginia Studies Teacher
Ritchie County Middle School

CAPSTONE
HIGH/LOW BOOKS
an imprint of Capstone Press

# C A P S T O N E    P R E S S

818 North Willow Street • Mankato, Minnesota 56001

http://www.capstone-press.com

*Library of Congress Cataloging-in-Publication Data*
Kummer, Patricia K.
    West Virginia/by Patricia K. Kummer (Capstone Press Geography Department).
       p. cm.--(One nation)
    Includes bibliographical references and index.
    Summary: Provides an overview of the Mountain State, including its
history, geography, people, and living conditions.
    ISBN 1-56065-685-9
    1. West Virginia--Juvenile literature. [1. West Virginia.]
    I. Capstone Press. Geography Dept. II. Title. III. Series.
F241.3.K86 1998
975.4--dc21
                                   97-40349
                                      CIP
                                      AC

**Editorial Credits**: Editor, Martha E. Hillman; cover design and illustrations, Timothy
    Halldin; photo research, Michelle L. Norstad
**Photo Credits**:
David Davis, 23
Thomas R. Fletcher, 6, 15, 30
International Stock/Michael Ventura, 32
G. Alan Nelson, cover
One Mile Up, 4 (top)
Root Resources/Richard Jacobs, 4 (bottom); Ruth A. Smith, 5 (bottom)
James P. Rowan, 35
Unicorn Stock Photos/Jean Higgins, 28
Visuals Unlimited/Arthur R. Hill, 10
West Virginia Division of Culture and History/Rick Lee, 25
West Virginia Division of Tourism, 26; Larry Belcher, 5(top); Stephen J. Shaluta Jr.,
    9, 16, 20, 36, 46

# Table of Contents

*Fast Facts about West Virginia* ..............................4

*Chapter 1* New River Gorge Bridge ....................7

*Chapter 2* The Land ..............................11

*Chapter 3* The People ...........................17

*Chapter 4* West Virginia History ......................21

*Chapter 5* West Virginia Business ....................29

*Chapter 6* Seeing the Sights ............................33


West Virginia Time Line....................................40

Famous West Virginians ......................................42

Words to Know ...................................................44

To Learn More ...................................................45

Internet Sites ......................................................46

Useful Addresses ...............................................47

Index ..................................................................48

# Fast Facts about West Virginia

**State Flag**

**Location:** In the southeastern United States

**Size:** 24,231 square miles (63,000 square kilometers)

**Population:** 1,825,754 (1996 U.S. Census Bureau estimate)

**Capital:** Charleston

**Cardinal**

**Date admitted to the Union:** June 20, 1863; the 35th state

**Rhododendron**

**Largest cities:** Charleston, Huntington, Wheeling, Parkersburg, Morgantown, Weirton, Fairmont, Beckley, Clarksburg, Martinsburg

**Nickname:** The Mountain State
**State animal:** Black bear
**State bird:** Cardinal
**State flower:** Rhododendron
**State tree:** Sugar maple

**Sugar maple**

**State songs:** "This Is My West Virginia," "West Virginia, My Home Sweet Home," and "The West Virginia Hills"

# Chapter 1
# New River Gorge Bridge

The New River Gorge Bridge in West Virginia is one of the world's longest bridges. A gorge is a deep valley with steep, rocky walls. The bridge reaches 3,030 feet (924 meters) across New River Gorge near Fayetteville.

The New River Gorge Bridge is also the second-highest bridge in the United States. It is 876 feet (267 meters) above the New River. Only the Royal Gorge Bridge in Colorado is higher.

## New River Gorge Bridge Day

Every October, West Virginians celebrate New River Gorge Bridge Day. This is West Virginia's

The New River Gorge Bridge rises above the New River.

largest one-day festival. A festival is a celebration held at the same time each year.

On that day, two of the bridge's four lanes are closed to cars. People walk on the bridge. They listen to music and enjoy good food. They buy arts and crafts made in West Virginia.

Every year, more than 400 BASE jumpers jump off the bridge wearing parachutes. BASE stands for Building, Antenna, Span, and Earth. BASE jumpers are people who parachute from tall buildings, towers, bridges, gorges, or mountains. A parachute is a large piece of strong, light cloth. A parachute lets a jumper float slowly and safely to the ground.

Other adventurers attach ropes from the bridge's arch to the gorge's side. Then they rappel from the bridge to the gorge. Rappel means to slide down a strong rope.

### New River Gorge

The New River is the second-oldest river in the world. Scientists believe it started flowing 65 million years ago. Only the Nile River in Africa is older.

**People enjoy white-water rafting in the New River Gorge.**

Between Fayetteville and Hinton, the New River carved a deep gorge. The walls of the gorge rise 1,440 feet (439 meters) above the river.

## Adventures in the New River Gorge

The New River Gorge is a popular place for white-water rafting. White-water rafting means steering a small boat through fast-moving water.

Rock climbers climb the gorge's walls. The Endless Wall is a popular climbing place. The wall is 150 feet (46 meters) high.

# Chapter 2
# The Land

West Virginia is in the southeastern United States. It is the only state with two panhandles. A panhandle is a narrow area of land that sticks out from a larger land area. On a map, it looks like the handle of a frying pan.

The Eastern Panhandle is between Maryland and Virginia. The Northern Panhandle pushes up between Pennsylvania and Ohio. Maryland, Virginia, Pennsylvania, Ohio, and Kentucky border West Virginia.

## The Mountain State

West Virginia's nickname is the Mountain State. It is in the Appalachian Mountains. West Virginia has few areas of flat land.

**West Virginia's nickname is the Mountain State.**

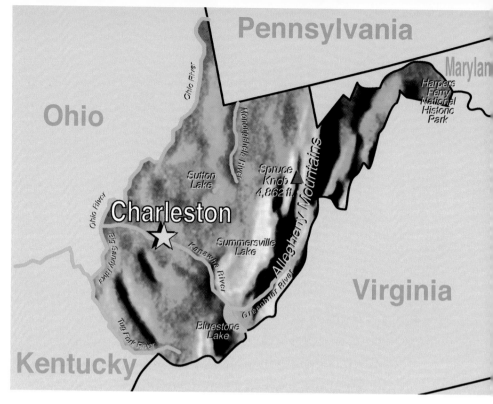

The Allegheny Mountains are part of the Appalachians in eastern West Virginia. West Virginia's highest point is Spruce Knob. It is in the Allegheny Mountains. Spruce Knob is 4,862 feet (1,482 meters) above sea level. Sea level is the average level of the ocean's surface.

### The Appalachian Plateau

The Appalachian Plateau covers the rest of the state. A plateau is an area of high, level land. Coal, oil, and natural gas lie under this plateau.

Some of West Virginia's longest rivers cut through the plateau. The state's largest cities are in the river valleys.

## Rivers and Cities

Long rivers flow through the southern part of the Appalachian Plateau. They include the Greenbrier, New, and Kanawha Rivers. Charleston is along the Kanawha. It is the state capital and the state's largest city.

Major rivers also run through the northern part of the Appalachian Plateau. They include the Cheat, Tygart, and Monongahela Rivers. Morgantown and Fairmont are two cities along the Monongahela River.

The Ohio River separates West Virginia from Ohio. Weirton, Wheeling, Parkersburg, and Huntington are large West Virginia cities along the Ohio River.

## Other Border Rivers

Other rivers also form West Virginia's borders. The Potomac River flows between West Virginia and Maryland. The state's lowest point is along this river at Harpers Ferry. It is 240 feet (73 meters) above sea level.

The Big Sandy and Tug Fork Rivers flow along southwestern West Virginia. They separate the state from Kentucky.

## Lakes

People made West Virginia's largest lakes when they built dams. Water from rivers backed up behind the dams. The water formed the lakes. These lakes include Sutton, Bluestone, Tygart, Summersville, and Stonewall Jackson Lakes.

Every fall, the U.S. Army opens the Summersville Dam at Summersville Lake. Water then rushes down the Gauley River. Rapids form on the river. People enjoy white-water rafting there.

## Woods and Wildlife

Forests cover much of West Virginia. Walnut, oak, and red spruce trees grow in these forests.

Black bears and deer live in West Virginia's wooded mountains. Bass and trout swim in its

**Summersville Lake is one of West Virginia's largest lakes.**

rivers. Hawks fly above Hawks Nest State
Park. Bald eagles live along the Potomac River.

## Climate

West Virginia has warm, wet summers. In
1996, West Virginia received almost 60 inches
(152 centimeters) of rain.

West Virginia winters are usually cool.
Mountain temperatures are colder than river
valley temperatures. The mountains also can
receive 100 inches (254 centimeters) of snow.

# Chapter 3
## The People

West Virginians call themselves mountaineers. A mountaineer is someone who climbs or lives in the mountains.

There are many advantages to living in West Virginia. It has a low crime rate. West Virginians pay less for goods and services than many other Americans.

But life can be hard in the Mountain State. West Virginians earn less money than people in most other states. West Virginia also has a high number of people without jobs. In 1996, about seven percent of West Virginians did not have jobs.

**A mountaineer is someone who climbs or lives in the mountains.**

Almost 64 percent of West Virginians live in rural areas. Rural means away from large cities and towns. Some live in small towns. Others own farms in the state's river valleys.

## European Ethnic Groups

About 96 percent of West Virginians have European backgrounds. Some of their families were among the state's first settlers.

The first European settlers came to the West Virginia area in 1727 from Pennsylvania. These Germans settlers founded Shepherdstown.

More settlers arrived in the late 1700s. Some came from England, Ireland, and Germany. Other settlers came from Virginia, Maryland, and New England. Most of their families were English, Scottish, Irish, or Dutch.

Between 1880 and the 1920s, more Europeans arrived. They included Italians, Poles, Austrians, and Hungarians. Most of them worked in the state's coal mines.

## African Americans

Some of West Virginia's first African Americans were slaves. They arrived in the early 1700s and worked on plantations. A plantation is a large farm. Some slaves traveled to the area in the 1780s with European explorers. By 1860, about 3,000 free African Americans lived there.

By 1910, about 61,000 African Americans were West Virginians. Many of them worked in the state's coal mines.

Today, about 57,000 West Virginians are African Americans. Many live in Charleston and Huntington.

## Other Ethnic Groups

Among the states, West Virginia has the smallest populations of three ethnic groups. They are Hispanic Americans, Asian Americans, and Native Americans.

Most West Virginia Hispanics have Mexican backgrounds. About 9,500 Hispanic Americans live in West Virginia.

About 8,700 Asian Americans are West Virginians. Indian Americans are West Virginia's largest Asian group.

Most Native Americans in West Virginia belong to the Cherokee nation. About 2,400 Native Americans live in the state.

# Chapter 4
# West Virginia History

West Virginia's first people arrived about 15,000 years ago. Adena people lived there between 3,000 and 1,000 years ago. They built dirt burial mounds in the Ohio, Potomac, and Kanawha Valleys. By 1600, Cherokee, Delaware, and Shawnee people hunted, farmed, and fished in West Virginia.

## American Explorers and Settlers
In 1607, England founded Virginia. This was the first of its 13 American colonies. The land that is now West Virginia was part of Virginia.

In the late 1600s, explorers from Virginia entered western Virginia. They explored the Eastern Panhandle and the New River area.

**Adena people built dirt burial mounds in river valleys.**

Settlers from other colonies arrived in the early 1700s. They built homes and farms. Most of them lived in the Eastern and Northern Panhandles.

By 1775, the U.S. government had forced Native Americans out of western Virginia. This opened the land between the Alleghenies and the Ohio River for settlement by colonists.

## The Revolutionary War

The Revolutionary War began in 1775. The colonies fought against England in this war. In 1776, the 13 American colonies declared their independence from England. Western Virginians fought English forces in the Ohio and Kanawha Valleys.

In 1783, the war ended. The colonies won their independence. They became the United States of America.

## Growth of Western Virginia

By 1800, about 79,000 people lived in western Virginia. Most of them had small farms.

Manufacturing businesses also flourished all over the state. Iron factories grew in the

Northern Panhandle. Companies produced salt and natural gas near Charleston. Grain mills produced flour.

## Slavery, Civil War, and Statehood

By 1860, slavery had divided the nation. The northern states had outlawed slavery. The southern states wanted to decide for themselves about slavery.

In 1861, Virginia seceded from the United States. Secede means to break away from a

**Grain mills produced flour in the 1800s.**

group. Ten other southern states also seceded. Together, they formed a new nation called the Confederate States of America. This led to the Civil War (1861-1865).

Many people in western Virginia opposed slavery. They did not want to secede from the United States. Instead, they voted to break away from Virginia. In 1863, western Virginia became the state of West Virginia.

The new state joined with Northern states to win the Civil War. After the war ended, the U.S. government freed all slaves in the nation.

## Growth in the New State

In the late 1800s, people built railroads throughout the state. The railroads carried coal from West Virginia mines to other states. They also hauled wood from the state's forests.

Chemical, glass, and steel businesses grew in the Ohio Valley. Between 1906 and 1924, West Virginia produced more natural gas than any other state.

## Labor Unions

Many West Virginians worked in coal mines during the early 1900s. Work in mines was hard

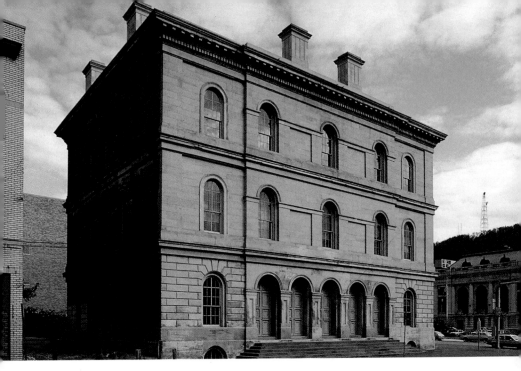

**West Virginians voted to break away from Virginia in the West Virginia Independence Hall.**

and dangerous. Explosions killed hundreds of miners. Workers began to form labor unions. A labor union is an organized group of workers. Union officials work to improve working conditions and salaries for workers.

In 1902, the United Mine Workers union started organizing West Virginia's miners. Mine owners opposed the union. Between 1912 and 1921, some armed fights occurred. Company guards and miners sometimes killed one another. Mine owners treated union members

**The need for coal has affected most of West Virginia's growth.**

poorly until 1933. In 1933, the U.S. government forced mine owners to let workers join unions.

## World Wars and Depression

In 1917, the United States entered World War I (1914-1918). West Virginia coal fueled the U.S. military and the rest of the country. Many West Virginians fought in the war.

Factories and mines closed all over the United States during the Great Depression

(1929-1939). Thousands of people lost their jobs. The U.S. government started a program called the New Deal. This program created jobs. Many West Virginians got jobs building new roads.

In 1941, the United States entered World War II (1939-1945). Factories and mines reopened. West Virginia coal again fueled the U.S. military. The military also used West Virginia steel and chemicals to make weapons for the war.

## Recent Challenges

The need for coal has affected most of West Virginia's growth during the past 50 years. Miners lost their jobs when the need for coal was low. Thousands of West Virginians left the state.

Sometimes the need for coal was high. Mines reopened during these times. People moved to West Virginia for mining jobs.

In the 1990s, companies from other states and countries came to West Virginia. The state's population grew again.

# Chapter 5
# West Virginia Business

West Virginia's best known business is coal mining. Manufacturing and agriculture are also important in West Virginia.

Service businesses are the state's largest businesses. Service businesses include transportation, trade, and tourism.

## Mining
West Virginians mine many products. Pipes carry natural gas from fields in western West Virginia. Oil comes from wells in the northwest. Salt comes from mines in Marshall County in the Northern Panhandle.

**Agriculture is an important West Virginia business.**

**Factories in the Ohio River Valley make glassware.**

West Virginia is a leading coal-mining state. Coal lies under two-thirds of its land. Many of the state's mines are in southern West Virginia.

More mining is now done by machines. Many coal miners have lost their jobs. This contributes to high unemployment in West Virginia.

## Manufacturing

Chemicals are major manufactured goods in West Virginia. Charleston and Parkersburg have many chemical factories.

Companies produce steel in Wheeling and Weirton. Factories in the Ohio River Valley make glassware. Paper companies make paper in the eastern mountains.

## Agriculture

Beef cattle are the state's most valuable farm product. Farmers raise cattle in river valleys on the Appalachian Plateau.

Farmers grow hay, corn, and tobacco mainly in the Ohio River Valley. Apples grow in the Eastern Panhandle.

## Service Industries

Transportation and trade are important businesses in West Virginia. Transportation means ways of moving people and objects from place to place. Huntington is the second busiest port along the Ohio River. People ship coal, chemicals, and other goods from this port.

Tourism is another big service industry. Every year, tourists spend about $4 billion in West Virginia. Tourists spend money at stores, motels, and state parks. They also spend money at festivals like New River Gorge Bridge Day.

# *Chapter 6*
# Seeing the Sights

West Virginia has many places to visit. People enjoy its mountains, woods, and rivers. Some visitors buy crafts at small town festivals. Others tour steel mills or glass factories.

## The Eastern Panhandle

West Virginia's first town was built in the Eastern Panhandle. This is Shepherdstown.

Berkeley Springs is the nation's oldest spa. A spa is a place where people bathe in spring water.

Harpers Ferry National Historical Park is southeast of Shepherdstown. In 1859, John Brown raided the U.S. arsenal there. An arsenal

John Brown raided the U.S. arsenal at Harpers Ferry.

is a place where weapons are stored. Brown tried to steal weapons and lead a slave rebellion. A rebellion is a fight against the people in charge. But the rebellion did not happen. Today, visitors can learn about Brown's raid.

## The Potomac Highlands

The Monongahela National Forest covers most of the Potomac Highlands in northeastern West Virginia. The Potomac River starts in this forest.

The cliff called Seneca Rocks is also in the forest. Seneca Rocks is 960 feet (293 meters) high. Rock climbers climb straight up this cliff. Other people walk along a twisting trail to the top.

Elkins is west of Seneca Rocks. Each October, the town hosts the State Championship Fiddle and Banjo Contest.

## North Central West Virginia

There is a two-lane covered bridge at Philippi. A covered bridge is an enclosed wooden bridge. This covered bridge is one of the few still used in the United States.

Each Labor Day, Clarksburg holds the Italian Heritage Festival. This is one of the largest festivals in West Virginia.

At nearby Fort New Salem, visitors learn about early German and Scotch-Irish settlers. These Scottish people once lived in Ireland. There are rebuilt log cabins at the fort.

Morgantown is home to West Virginia University. Its sports teams are called the Mountaineers.

**There is a two-lane covered bridge at Philippi.**

## Central West Virginia

Central West Virginia is known as the Mountain Lakes area. Scuba divers like the clear waters of Summersville Lake.

A steamboat called *Stonewall Jackson Paddlewheel* takes visitors around Stonewall Jackson Lake. Stonewall Jackson was a Confederate general.

## Southeastern West Virginia

Southeastern West Virginia has many caves. Organ Cave is one unusual cave. One of its rocks looks like a pipe organ.

The Beckley Exhibition Coal Mine is in Beckley. Retired miners lead tours through underground tunnels.

## Southwestern West Virginia

Charleston is in southwestern West Virginia. The capitol there has a tall golden dome. A dome is a roof shaped like half of a globe. The dome is 293 feet (89 meters) tall. It is five feet (1.5 meters) taller than the dome of the U.S. Capitol.

**The capitol in Charleston has a tall golden dome.**

Visitors tour the Blenko Glass Company in Milton. Until 1996, its workers made statues given to winners of the Country Music Award.

Huntington is on the Ohio River. The Huntington Museum of Art is there. Museum visitors see West Virginia art works and dishes.

## The Mid-Ohio River Valley

The Mid-Ohio River Valley also has many glass factories. Some of them produce marbles. In Pennsboro, workers make marbles by hand.

Parkersburg is along the Ohio River. Visitors can take a riverboat to Blennerhassett Island. Harman Blennerhassett was a wealthy businessman. He built a large house on the island in 1800. In 1806, Blennerhassett lost his fortune. The house burned down in 1811. Today, visitors tour the rebuilt house.

## The Northern Panhandle

West Virginia Independence Hall is in Wheeling. The people of western Virginia declared their independence from Virginia in this building.

Moundsville is south of Wheeling. About 2,000 years ago, Adena people built Grave Creek Mound there out of dirt. It is the nation's largest cone-shaped burial mound.

Newell is at West Virginia's far northern tip. The Homer Laughlin China Company is in Newell. Visitors can watch workers there make colorful dishes.

# West Virginia Time Line

**About 13,000 B.C.** —The first people arrive in the area that later became West Virginia.

**About 1,000 B.C.**—Mound builders are living in the Ohio and Kanawha River Valleys.

**A.D. 1600s**—Cherokee, Delaware, and Shawnee people are hunting in the West Virginia area.

**1607**—The English create Virginia, which is their first American colony. West Virginia is part of Virginia.

**1671-1673**—Virginians explore present-day West Virginia. They discover the New and Kanawha Rivers.

**1727**—German settlers from Pennsylvania set up present-day Shepherdstown.

**1742**—Coal is found along the Coal River.

**1768**—Native Americans leave the land between the Allegheny Mountains and the Ohio River.

**1775-1783**—People in western Virginia help the United States win its independence from England.

**1859**—John Brown raids Harpers Ferry.

**1861**—Virginia secedes from the Union; Virginia's western counties form West Virginia.

**1863**—West Virginia becomes the 35th state.

**1885**—Charleston becomes the permanent state capital.

**1912-1921**—Armed conflict occurs between coal miners and mine owners.

**1929-1939**—During the Great Depression, West Virginians receive jobs as part of the New Deal.

**1968**—A coal mine explosion in Farmington leads to new safety laws.

**1972**—A dam collapses, causing a flood that kills 125 people along Buffalo Creek.

**1989**—The West Virginia Mountaineers football team loses the NCAA Championship to Notre Dame in the Fiesta Bowl.

**1991**—West Virginia passes laws to improve education and protect its water.

**1996**—Wind and rain results in flooding and other damage in the Eastern Panhandle.

# Famous West Virginians

**Belle Boyd** (1843-1900) Spy for the Confederacy during the Civil War; later, wrote a book about her wartime experiences; born in Martinsburg.

**George Brett** (1953- ) Baseball player who was named the American League's Most Valuable Player (1980); led the Kansas City Royals to the World Series championship (1985); born in Glen Dale.

**Pearl S. Buck** (1892-1973) Author who grew up in China; won the Pulitzer Prize for *The Good Earth* (1932) and was awarded the Nobel Prize in literature (1938); born in Hillsboro.

**Henry Louis Gates, Jr.** (1950- ) Teacher and writer; wrote *Colored People: A Memoir* (1994), a book about growing up in West Virginia; born in Keyser and grew up in Piedmont.

**Mary Lou Retton** (1968- ) Gymnast who won a gold medal for her performance in the 1984 Olympic Games; born in Fairmont.

**Jay Rockefeller** (1937- ) Public servant and politician; served West Virginia as governor (1977-1985) and as a U.S. senator (1985- ); born in New York.

**Cyrus Vance** (1917- ) Lawyer and statesman; served as U.S. secretary of state for President Jimmy Carter (1977-1981); later worked to bring peace in Bosnia (1991-1993); born in Clarksburg.

**Jerry West** (1938- ) Basketball player who led the Los Angeles Lakers to the NBA Championship (1972); named to the Basketball Hall of Fame (1979); born in Cabin Creek.

**Chuck Yeager** (1923- ) First pilot to fly faster than the speed of sound (1947); Yeager Airport in Charleston is named after him; born in Myra.

# Words to Know

**arsenal** (AR-suh-nuhl)—a place where weapons are stored

**BASE jumpers** (BAYSS JUHM-purs)—Building, Antenna, Span, and Earth jumpers; people who parachute from tall buildings, towers, bridges, gorges, or mountains

**festival** (FESS-tuh-vuhl)—a celebration that is held at the same time each year

**gorge** (GORJ)—a deep valley with steep, rocky walls

**labor union** (LAY-bur YOON-yuhn)—an organized group of workers

**panhandle** (PAN-han-duhl)—a narrow area of land that sticks out from a larger land area; on a map, a panhandle looks like the handle of a frying pan.

**parachute** (PA-ruh-shoot)—a large piece of strong, light fabric; it allows a person jumping from a high place to float slowly and safely to the ground.

**plateau** (pla-TOH)—an area of high, level land

**rappel** (rah-PEL)—to slide down a strong rope

**rebellion** (ri-BEL-yuhn)—a fight against the people in charge

**rural** (RUR-uhl)—areas away from large cities and towns

**sea level** (SEE LEV-uhl)—the average level of the ocean's surface

**secede** (si-SEED)—to break away from a group

**white-water rafting** (WITE-WAH-tur RAF-ting)—steering a small boat through fast-moving water

# To Learn More

**Di Piazza, Domenica**. *West Virginia*. Hello U.S.A. Minneapolis: Lerner, 1995.

**Fradin, Dennis B. and Judith Bloom Fradin**. *West Virginia*. From Sea to Shining Sea. Chicago: Children's Press, 1994.

**Tackach, James**. *The Trial of John Brown*. San Diego: Lucent Books, 1998.

**Thompson, Kathleen**. *West Virginia*. Austin, Tex.: Raintree Steck-Vaughn, 1996.

# Internet Sites

**City.Net West Virginia, United States**
http://city.net/countries/united_states/west_virginia

**TRAVEL.org—West Virginia**
http://travel.org/westvirg.html

**West Virginia—It's You!**
http://www.westvirginia.com

**West Virginia State Symbols**
http://www.wvauditor.com/wvinfo/wvinfo2.html

Seneca Rocks is a popular place for rock climbing.

# Useful Addresses

**Beckley Exhibition Coal Mine**
Drawer AJ
Beckley, WV 25802

**Harpers Ferry National Historical Park**
National Park Service
P.O. Box 65
Harpers Ferry, WV 25425

**Monongahela National Forest**
U.S. Forest Service
200 Sycamore Street
Elkins, WV 26241

**West Virginia Division of Tourism**
PO Box 50312
Charleston, WV 25305

**West Virginia Independence Hall**
16th and Market Streets
Wheeling, WV 26003

# Index

African Americans, 18-19
Allegheny Mountains, 12
Appalachian Plateau, 12-13, 31
Asian Americans, 19

BASE jumpers, 8

Charleston, 13, 19, 23, 30, 37
Civil War, 23-24
climate, 15
coal, 12, 18, 19, 24, 26, 27, 29, 30, 31, 37

Eastern Panhandle, 11, 21, 31, 33-34

Grave Creek Mound, 39
Great Depression, 26

Harpers Ferry, 14, 33
Hispanic Americans, 19

Kanawha River, 13

manufacturing, 22, 29, 30-31
mine, 18, 19, 24, 25, 26, 27, 29, 30, 37
mountaineer, 17
Mountain State, 11-12, 17

Native Americans, 19, 22
New River, 7, 8, 9, 21
New River Gorge Bridge, 8, 31
Northern Panhandle, 11, 22, 23, 28, 38-39

parachute, 8
Potomac River, 13, 15, 34

rappel, 8

secede, 23, 24
spring water, 33

tourism, 29, 31

white-water rafting, 9, 14